Soon To Be Mrs. & Mrs.

Wedding Date:

Wedding Planner

WEDDING DATE & TIME:

VENUE ADDRESS:

BUDGET:

OFFICIANT:

WEDDING PARTY:

TO DO LIST:

NOTES & REMINDERS:

Wedding Budget Planner

	TOTAL COST:	DEPOSIT:	REMAINDER:
WEDDING VENUE			
RECEPTION VENUE			
FLORIST			
OFFICIANT			
CATERER			
WEDDING CAKE			
BRIDAL ATTIRE (1ST)			
BRIDAL ATTIRE (2ND)			
BRIDAL JEWELRY			
BRIDESMAIDS ATTIRE			
USHERS ATTIRE			
HAIR & MAKE UP			
PHOTOGRAPHER			
VIDEOGRAPHER			
DJ SERVICE/ENTERTAINMENT			
INVITATIONS			
TRANSPORTATION			
WEDDING PARTY GIFTS			
RENTALS			
HONEYMOON			

Additional Budget Planner

	TOTAL COST:	DEPOSIT:	REMAINDER:

12 Months Before

- SET THE DATE
- SET YOUR BUDGET
- CHOOSE YOUR THEME
- ORGANIZE ENGAGEMENT PARTY
- RESEARCH VENUES
- BOOK A WEDDING PLANNER
- RESEARCH PHOTOGRAPHERS
- RESEARCH VIDEOGRAPHERS
- RESEARCH DJ'S/ENTERTAINMENT

- CONSIDER FLORISTS
- RESEARCH CATERERS
- DECIDE ON OFFICIANT
- CREATE INITIAL GUEST LIST
- CHOOSE WEDDING PARTY
- SHOP FOR WEDDING DRESSES AND/OR BRIDAL SUITS
- REGISTER WITH GIFT REGISTRY
- DISCUSS HONEYMOON IDEAS
- RESEARCH WEDDING RINGS

THINGS TO REMEMBER:

Additional Notes

9 Months Before

- FINALIZE GUEST LIST
- ORDER INVITATIONS
- PLAN YOUR RECEPTION
- BOOK PHOTOGRAPHER
- BOOK VIDEOGRAPHER
- BOOK FLORIST
- BOOK DJ/ENTERTAINMENT
- BOOK CATERER
- CHOOSE WEDDING CAKE

- CHOOSE WEDDING ATTIRE (DRESS AND/OR BRIDAL SUIT)
- ORDER BRIDESMAIDS DRESSES
- RESERVE TUXEDOS
- ARRANGE TRANSPORTATION
- BOOK WEDDING VENUE
- BOOK RECEPTION VENUE
- PLAN HONEYMOON
- BOOK OFFICIANT
- BOOK ROOMS FOR GUESTS

THINGS TO REMEMBER:

Additional Notes

6 Months Before

- ORDER THANK YOU NOTES
- REVIEW RECEPTION DETAILS
- MAKE APPT'S FOR THE DRESS/BRIDAL SUIT FITTINGS
- CONFIRM BRIDEMAIDS DRESSES
- GET MARRIAGE LICENSE

- BOOK HAIR/MAKE UP STYLISTS
- CONFIRM MUSIC SELECTIONS
- PLAN BRIDAL SHOWERS
- PLAN REHEARSAL
- SHOP FOR WEDDING RINGS

THINGS TO REMEMBER:

Additional Notes

3 Months Before

- MAIL OUT INVITATIONS
- MEET WITH OFFICIANT
- BUY GIFTS FOR WEDDING PARTY
- BOOK FINAL GOWN/BRIDAL SUIT FITTINGS
- BUY WEDDING BANDS
- PLAN YOUR HAIR STYLES
- PURCHASE SHOES/HEELS
- CONFIRM PASSPORTS ARE VALID

- FINALIZE RECEPTION MENU
- PLAN REHEARSAL DINNER
- CONFIRM ALL BOOKINGS
- APPLY FOR MARRIAGE LICENSE
- CONFIRM MUSIC SELECTIONS
- DRAFT WEDDING VOWS
- CHOOSE YOUR MC
- ARRANGE AIRPORT TRANSFER

THINGS TO REMEMBER:

Additional Notes

1 Month Before

- CONFIRM FINAL GUEST COUNT
- CONFIRM RECEPTION DETAILS
- ATTEND FINAL GOWN/BRIDAL SUIT FITTINGS
- CONFIRM PHOTOGRAPHER
- WRAP WEDDING PARTY GIFTS
- CREATE PHOTOGRAPHY SHOT LIST

- REHEARSE WEDDING VOWS
- BOOK MANI'S-PEDI'S
- CONFIRM WITH FLORIST
- CONFIRM VIDEOGRAPHER
- PICK UP BRIDEMAIDS DRESSES
- CREATE WEDDING SCHEDULE

THINGS TO REMEMBER:

Additional Notes

1 Week Before

- FINALIZE SEATING PLANS
- MAKE PAYMENTS TO VENDORS
- PACK FOR HONEYMOON
- CONFIRM HOTEL RESERVATIONS
- GIVE SCHEDULE TO PARTY

- DELIVER LICENSE TO OFFICIANT
- CONFIRM WITH BAKERY
- PICK UP WEDDING DRESSES/BRIDAL SUITS
- PICK UP TUXEDOS
- GIVE MUSIC LIST TO DJ

THINGS TO REMEMBER:

Additional Notes

1 Day Before

- GET MANICURE'S/PEDICURE'S
- ATTEND REHEARSAL DINNER
- GET A GOOD NIGHT'S SLEEP!

- GIVE GIFTS TO WEDDING PARTY
- FINALIZE PACKING

TO DO LIST:

Additional Notes

The Big Day!

- [ ] GET HAIR & MAKE UP DONE
- [ ] HAVE A HEALTHY BREAKFAST
- [ ] ENJOY YOUR BIG DAY!

- [ ] MEET WITH BRIDESMAIDS AND/OR USHERS
- [ ] GIVE RINGS TO HONOR ATTENDANTS

TO DO LIST:

Wedding Planner

JOINT ENGAGEMENT PARTY:

DATE: _____   LOCATION: _____

TIME: _____   NUMBER OF GUESTS: _____

NOTES:

BRIDAL SHOWER 1:

DATE: _____   LOCATION: _____

TIME: _____   NUMBER OF GUESTS: _____

NOTES:

BRIDAL SHOWER 2:

DATE: _____   LOCATION: _____

TIME: _____   NUMBER OF GUESTS: _____

NOTES:

Wedding Party

1ST BRIDE'S MAID/MATRON OF HONOR/BEST WOMAN:

PHONE: _____ DRESS SIZE: _____ SHOE SIZE: _____

EMAIL: _____

BRIDESMAID:

PHONE: _____ DRESS SIZE: _____ SHOE SIZE: _____

EMAIL: _____

BRIDESMAID #2:

PHONE: _____ DRESS SIZE: _____ SHOE SIZE: _____

EMAIL: _____

BRIDESMAID #3:

PHONE: _____ DRESS SIZE: _____ SHOE SIZE: _____

EMAIL: _____

BRIDESMAID #4:

PHONE: _____ DRESS SIZE: _____ SHOE SIZE: _____

EMAIL: _____

NOTES:

Wedding Party

2ND BRIDE'S MAID/MATRON OF HONOR/BEST WOMAN:

PHONE: _____ DRESS SIZE: _____ SHOE SIZE: _____

EMAIL: _____

BRIDESMAID:

PHONE: _____ DRESS SIZE: _____ SHOE SIZE: _____

EMAIL: _____

BRIDESMAID #2:

PHONE: _____ DRESS SIZE: _____ SHOE SIZE: _____

EMAIL: _____

BRIDESMAID #3:

PHONE: _____ DRESS SIZE: _____ SHOE SIZE: _____

EMAIL: _____

BRIDESMAID #4:

PHONE: _____ DRESS SIZE: _____ SHOE SIZE: _____

EMAIL: _____

NOTES:

Additional Wedding Party

BEST MAN:

PHONE: _____ WAIST SIZE: _____ SHOE SIZE: _____

NECK SIZE: _____ SLEEVE SIZE: _____ JACKET SIZE: _____

EMAIL: _____

USHER #1:

PHONE: _____ WAIST SIZE: _____ SHOE SIZE: _____

NECK SIZE: _____ SLEEVE SIZE: _____ JACKET SIZE: _____

EMAIL: _____

USHER #2:

PHONE: _____ WAIST SIZE: _____ SHOE SIZE: _____

NECK SIZE: _____ SLEEVE SIZE: _____ JACKET SIZE: _____

EMAIL: _____

USHER #3:

PHONE: _____ WAIST SIZE: _____ SHOE SIZE: _____

NECK SIZE: _____ SLEEVE SIZE: _____ JACKET SIZE: _____

EMAIL: _____

USHER #4:

PHONE: _____ WAIST SIZE: _____ SHOE SIZE: _____

NECK SIZE: _____ SLEEVE SIZE: _____ JACKET SIZE: _____

EMAIL: _____

Photographer

PHOTOGRAPHER:

PHONE: _____   COMPANY: _____

EMAIL: _____   ADDRESS: _____

WEDDING PACKAGE OVERVIEW:

EST PRICE: _____

INCLUSIONS:	YES ✓	NO ✓	COST:
ENGAGEMENT SHOOT:	☐	☐	_____
PHOTO ALBUMS:	☐	☐	_____
FRAMES:	☐	☐	_____
PROOFS INCLUDED:	☐	☐	_____
NEGATIVES INCLUDED:	☐	☐	_____

TOTAL COST:

Videographer

VIDEOGRAPHER:

PHONE: .... COMPANY: ....

EMAIL: .... ADDRESS: ....

WEDDING PACKAGE OVERVIEW:

EST PRICE: ....

INCLUSIONS:	YES ✓	NO ✓	COST:
DUPLICATES/COPIES:	☐	☐	....
PHOTO MONTAGE:	☐	☐	....
MUSIC ADDED:	☐	☐	....
EDITING:	☐	☐	....

TOTAL COST: ....

NOTES:

DJ / Entertainment

DJ/LIVE BAND/ENTERTAINMENT:

PHONE: _____   COMPANY: _____

EMAIL: _____   ADDRESS: _____

START TIME: _____   END TIME: _____

ENTERTAINMENT SERVICE OVERVIEW:

EST PRICE: _____

INCLUSIONS:	YES ✓	NO ✓	COST:
SOUND EQUIPMENT:	☐	☐	_____
LIGHTING:	☐	☐	_____
SPECIAL EFFECTS:	☐	☐	_____
GRATUITIES	☐	☐	_____

TOTAL COST: _____

NOTES:

Florist

FLORIST:

PHONE: _____ COMPANY: _____

EMAIL: _____ ADDRESS: _____

FLORAL PACKAGE:

EST PRICE: _____

INCLUSIONS:	YES ✓	NO ✓	COST:
BRIDAL BOUQUET'S:	☐	☐	_____
THROW AWAY BOUQUET:	☐	☐	_____
CORSAGES:	☐	☐	_____
CEREMONY FLOWERS	☐	☐	_____
CENTERPIECES	☐	☐	_____
CAKE TOPPER	☐	☐	_____
BOUTONNIERE	☐	☐	_____

TOTAL COST:

Wedding Cake/Baker

PHONE: _____   COMPANY: _____

EMAIL: _____   ADDRESS: _____

WEDDING CAKE PACKAGE:

COST: _____   FREE TASTING: _____   DELIVERY FEE: _____

FLAVOR: _____

FILLING: _____

SIZE: _____

SHAPE: _____

COLOR: _____

EXTRAS: _____

TOTAL COST: _____

NOTES:

Transportation Planner

TO CEREMONY: PICK UP TIME: PICK UP LOCATION:

BRIDE 1:

BRIDE 2:

1ST BRIDE'S PARENTS:

2ST BRIDE'S PARENTS:

BRIDESMAIDS:

USHERS:

NOTES:

TO RECEPTION: PICK UP TIME: PICK UP LOCATION:

BRIDE & BRIDE:

1ST BRIDE'S PARENTS:

2ND BRIDE'S PARENTS:

BRIDESMAIDS:

USHERS:

Wedding Planner

BACHELORETTE PARTY 1:

DATE: _____   LOCATION: _____

TIME: _____   NUMBER OF GUESTS: _____

NOTES:

BACHELORETTE PARTY 2:

DATE: _____   LOCATION: _____

TIME: _____   NUMBER OF GUESTS: _____

NOTES:

CEREMONY REHEARSAL:

DATE: _____   LOCATION: _____

TIME: _____   NUMBER OF GUESTS: _____

NOTES:

Wedding Planner

REHEARSAL DINNER:

DATE: _____   LOCATION: _____

TIME: _____   NUMBER OF GUESTS: _____

NOTES:

RECEPTION:

DATE: _____   LOCATION: _____

TIME: _____   NUMBER OF GUESTS: _____

NOTES:

REMINDERS:

_____

_____

_____

_____

Names & Addresses

CEREMONY:

PHONE: _____   CONTACT NAME: _____

EMAIL: _____   ADDRESS: _____

RECEPTION:

PHONE: _____   CONTACT NAME: _____

EMAIL: _____   ADDRESS: _____

OFFICIANT:

PHONE: _____   CONTACT NAME: _____

EMAIL: _____   ADDRESS: _____

WEDDING PLANNER:

PHONE: _____   CONTACT NAME: _____

EMAIL: _____   ADDRESS: _____

CATERER:

PHONE: _____   CONTACT NAME: _____

EMAIL: _____   ADDRESS: _____

FLORIST:

PHONE: _____   CONTACT NAME: _____

EMAIL: _____   ADDRESS: _____

Names & Addresses

BAKERY:

PHONE: _____

EMAIL: _____

CONTACT NAME: _____

ADDRESS: _____

BRIDAL SHOP:

PHONE: _____

EMAIL: _____

CONTACT NAME: _____

ADDRESS: _____

PHOTOGRAPHER:

PHONE: _____

EMAIL: _____

CONTACT NAME: _____

ADDRESS: _____

VIDEOGRAPHER:

PHONE: _____

EMAIL: _____

CONTACT NAME: _____

ADDRESS: _____

DJ/ENTERTAINMENT:

PHONE: _____

EMAIL: _____

CONTACT NAME: _____

ADDRESS: _____

HAIR/NAIL SALON:

PHONE: _____

EMAIL: _____

CONTACT NAME: _____

ADDRESS: _____

Names & Addresses

MAKE UP ARTIST:

PHONE: _____

CONTACT NAME: _____

EMAIL: _____

ADDRESS: _____

RENTALS:

PHONE: _____

CONTACT NAME: _____

EMAIL: _____

ADDRESS: _____

HONEYMOON RESORT/HOTEL:

PHONE: _____

CONTACT NAME: _____

EMAIL: _____

ADDRESS: _____

TRANSPORTATION SERVICE:

PHONE: _____

CONTACT NAME: _____

EMAIL: _____

ADDRESS: _____

NOTES:

Caterer Details

CONTACT INFORMATION:

PHONE: _____

CONTACT NAME: _____

EMAIL: _____

ADDRESS: _____

MENU CHOICE #1:

MENU CHOICE #2:

	YES ✓	NO ✓	COST:
BAR INCLUDED:			_____
CORKAGE FEE:			_____
HORS D'OEUVRES:			_____
TAXES INCLUDED:			_____
GRATUITIES INCLUDED:			_____

Menu Planner

HORS D'OEUVRES

1st COURSE:

2nd COURSE:

3rd COURSE:

4th COURSE:

DESSERT:

1 Week Before

	THINGS TO DO:	NOTES:
MONDAY		
TUESDAY		
WEDNESDAY		
THURSDAY		

REMINDERS & NOTES:

1 Week Before

	THINGS TO DO:	NOTES:
FRIDAY		
SATURDAY		
SUNDAY		

LEFT TO DO:

REMINDERS:

NOTES:

Additional Notes

Wedding Guest List

NAME:	ADDRESS:	# IN PARTY:	RSVP: ✓

Wedding Guest List

NAME:	ADDRESS:	# IN PARTY:	RSVP: ✓

Wedding Guest List

NAME:	ADDRESS:	# IN PARTY:	RSVP: ✓

Wedding Guest List

NAME:	ADDRESS:	# IN PARTY:	RSVP: ✓

Wedding Guest List

NAME:	ADDRESS:	# IN PARTY:	RSVP: ✓

Wedding Guest List

NAME:	ADDRESS:	# IN PARTY:	RSVP: ✓

Wedding Guest List

NAME:	ADDRESS:	# IN PARTY:	RSVP: ✓

Wedding Guest List

NAME:	ADDRESS:	# IN PARTY:	RSVP: ✓

Wedding Guest List

NAME:	ADDRESS:	# IN PARTY:	RSVP: ✓

Wedding Guest List

NAME:	ADDRESS:	# IN PARTY:	RSVP: ✓

Wedding Guest List

NAME:	ADDRESS:	# IN PARTY:	RSVP: ✓

Wedding Guest List

NAME:	ADDRESS:	# IN PARTY:	RSVP: ✓

Wedding Guest List

NAME:	ADDRESS:	# IN PARTY:	RSVP: ✓

Wedding Guest List

NAME:	ADDRESS:	# IN PARTY:	RSVP: ✓

Wedding Guest List

NAME:	ADDRESS:	# IN PARTY:	RSVP: ✓

Wedding Guest List

NAME:	ADDRESS:	# IN PARTY:	RSVP: ✓

Wedding Guest List

NAME:	ADDRESS:	# IN PARTY:	RSVP: ✓

Wedding Guest List

NAME:	ADDRESS:	# IN PARTY:	RSVP: ✓

Wedding Guest List

NAME:	ADDRESS:	# IN PARTY:	RSVP: ✓

Wedding Guest List

NAME:	ADDRESS:	# IN PARTY:	RSVP: ✓

Wedding Guest List

NAME:	ADDRESS:	# IN PARTY:	RSVP: ✓

Wedding Guest List

NAME:	ADDRESS:	# IN PARTY:	RSVP: ✓

Wedding Guest List

NAME:	ADDRESS:	# IN PARTY:	RSVP: ✓

Wedding Guest List

NAME:	ADDRESS:	# IN PARTY:	RSVP: ✓

Wedding Guest List

NAME:	ADDRESS:	# IN PARTY:	RSVP: ✓

Wedding Guest List

NAME:	ADDRESS:	# IN PARTY:	RSVP: ✓

Wedding Guest List

NAME:	ADDRESS:	# IN PARTY:	RSVP: ✓

Wedding Guest List

NAME:	ADDRESS:	# IN PARTY:	RSVP: ✓

Wedding Guest List

NAME:	ADDRESS:	# IN PARTY:	RSVP: ✓

Wedding Guest List

NAME:	ADDRESS:	# IN PARTY:	RSVP: ✓

Wedding Guest List

NAME:	ADDRESS:	# IN PARTY:	RSVP: ✓

Wedding Guest List

NAME:	ADDRESS:	# IN PARTY:	RSVP: ✓

Wedding Guest List

NAME:	ADDRESS:	# IN PARTY:	RSVP: ✓

Wedding Guest List

NAME:	ADDRESS:	# IN PARTY:	RSVP: ✓

Wedding Guest List

NAME:	ADDRESS:	# IN PARTY:	RSVP: ✓

Wedding Guest List

NAME:	ADDRESS:	# IN PARTY:	RSVP: ✓

Wedding Guest List

NAME:	ADDRESS:	# IN PARTY:	RSVP: ✓

Wedding Guest List

NAME:	ADDRESS:	# IN PARTY:	RSVP: ✓

Wedding Guest List

NAME:	ADDRESS:	# IN PARTY:	RSVP: ✓

Wedding Guest List

NAME:	ADDRESS:	# IN PARTY:	RSVP: ✓

Wedding Guest List

NAME:	ADDRESS:	# IN PARTY:	RSVP: ✓

Wedding Guest List

NAME:	ADDRESS:	# IN PARTY:	RSVP: ✓

Seating Chart Planner

Table #

Table #

Table #

Table #

SEATING PLANNER NOTES:

Seating Chart Planner

Table #

Table #

Table #

Table #

SEATING PLANNER NOTES:

Seating Chart Planner

Table #

Table #

Table #

Table #

SEATING PLANNER NOTES:

Seating Chart Planner

Table #

Table #

Table #

Table #

SEATING PLANNER NOTES:

Seating Chart Planner

Table #

Table #

Table #

Table #

SEATING PLANNER NOTES:

Seating Chart Planner

Table #

Table #

Table #

Table #

SEATING PLANNER NOTES:

Seating Chart Planner

Table #

Table #

Table #

Table #

SEATING PLANNER NOTES:

Seating Chart Planner

Table #

Table #

Table #

Table #

SEATING PLANNER NOTES:

Seating Chart Planner

Table #

Table #

Table #

Table #

SEATING PLANNER NOTES:

Seating Chart Planner

Table #

Table #

Table #

Table #

SEATING PLANNER NOTES:

Seating Chart Planner

Table #

Table #

Table #

Table #

SEATING PLANNER NOTES:

Seating Chart Planner

Table #

Table #

Table #

Table #

SEATING PLANNER NOTES:

Seating Chart Planner

Table #

Table #

Table #

Table #

SEATING PLANNER NOTES:

Seating Chart Planner

Table #

Table #

Table #

Table #

SEATING PLANNER NOTES:

Seating Chart Planner

Table #

Table #

Table #

Table #

SEATING PLANNER NOTES:

Seating Chart Planner

Table #

Table #

Table #

Table #

SEATING PLANNER NOTES:

Seating Chart Planner

Table #

Table #

Table #

Table #

SEATING PLANNER NOTES:

Seating Chart Planner

Table #

Table #

Table #

Table #

SEATING PLANNER NOTES:

Seating Chart Planner

Table #

Table #

Table #

Table #

SEATING PLANNER NOTES:

Seating Chart Planner

Table #

Table #

Table #

Table #

SEATING PLANNER NOTES:

Seating Chart Planner

Table #

Table #

Table #

Table #

SEATING PLANNER NOTES:

Seating Chart Planner

Table #

Table #

Table #

Table #

SEATING PLANNER NOTES:

Seating Chart Planner

Table #

Table #

Table #

Table #

SEATING PLANNER NOTES:

Seating Chart Planner

Table #

Table #

Table #

Table #

SEATING PLANNER NOTES:

Seating Chart Planner

Table #

Table #

Table #

Table #

SEATING PLANNER NOTES:

Seating Chart Planner

Table #

Table #

Table #

Table #

SEATING PLANNER NOTES:

Seating Chart Planner

Table #

Table #

Table #

Table #

SEATING PLANNER NOTES:

Seating Chart Planner

Table #

Table #

Table #

Table #

SEATING PLANNER NOTES:

♥ Notes ♥

♥ Notes ♥

♥ Notes ♥

Notes

♥ Notes ♥

♥ Notes ♥

♥ Notes ♥

 Notes

# ♥ Notes ♥

♥ Notes ♥

♥ Notes ♥

♥ Notes ♥

Notes

♥ Notes ♥

♥ Notes ♥

♥ Notes ♥

♥ Notes ♥

Made in the USA
Monee, IL
16 September 2020